WHAT'S IT LIKE TO BE A..?

TV
PRODUCER

Elizabeth Dowen   Lisa Thompson

First published in the UK 2009 by
A & C Black Publishing Ltd
36 Soho Square
London
W1D 3QY
www.acblack.com

Copyright © 2009 Blake Publishing
Published 2008 by Blake Education Pty Ltd, Australia

ISBN: 978-1-4081-1425-4

A CIP catalogue record for this book is available from the British Library.

Written by Lisa Thompson and Elizabeth Dowen
Publisher: Katy Pike
Series Editor: Eve Tonelli
Cover Design: Terry Woodley
Designer: D Brown and Clifford Hayes
Printed in Singapore by Tien Wah Press.

Cover image © Dennis MacDonald/Alamy

All inside images © Shutterstock except p. 41 (br) (aap)

This book is produced using paper made from wood grown in managed,
sustainable forests. It is natural, renewable and recyclable. The logging and
manufacturing processes conform to the environmental regulations of the
country of origin.

All the Internet addresses given in this book were correct at the time of
going to press. The author and publishers regret any inconvenience caused
if addresses have changed or sites have ceased to exist, but can accept no
responsibility for any such changes.

Contents

Working as a TV Producer

Monday
6 am - travel to Longleat Wildlife Park
All day - location shoot for Purple Lava at Longleat Wildlife Park

Tuesday
9 am - meeting with my executive producer to go over budgets and possible pilot schedules for Monster TV
1 pm - meeting with Purple Lava researchers about list of guests for show next week
Afternoon - check final scripts for tomorrow's studio filming of Purple Lava

Wednesday
8 am - start studio filming day for Purple Lava

Thursday
10 am - casting for presenters of Monster TV with director
2 pm - meet with graphics team about Monster TV titles and marketing team about promotional material
4 pm - meeting with writers of Monster TV

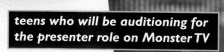

teens who will be auditioning for the presenter role on Monster TV

MY JOB

As a TV producer, I am the member of the production team who guides a project from beginning to end – that is, from the initial idea to finding funding, budgets, scripting, filming, editing and final distribution. It is a producer's role to make sure the project runs smoothly, comes in on budget, reaches its target audience and is successfully completed.

budgets, scripts, proposals

Friday
Check final edit for Purple Lava location footage to go to air Saturday morning.

Go over production and shooting schedule for Monster TV pilot

DIDYOUKNOW?

THE ORIGINS OF TELEVISION

The word *television* comes from the Greek word *tele*, meaning *far* and the Latin word *visio* meaning *vision* or *sight*.

MONDAY

It's not even 7 am and already my mobile has been ringing non stop for the last half-hour. My programme, Purple Lava — which is a children's programme with interviews, cartoons and dares, hosted by three teenagers — is scheduled to film segments on-location at a wildlife park. However, the camera crew have been delayed due to traffic chaos on the motorway. They'll now be late joining us on-location and this affects our tight filming schedule. As all filming must be done today, due to budget and time constraints, I am now trying to juggle our filming schedule with park staff.

I am sipping my morning coffee on the minibus to the wildlife park as I go over the scripts for the presenters. I am ready for whatever is in store — and after years working as a producer in TV, I know things rarely, if ever, go as planned. When I was starting out in the industry, someone once told me, "The key to survival as a producer is always be prepared, remember everything can be negotiated and laugh often!" That was excellent advice!

Our film crew is late!

How do I look?

A producer always needs to read and re-read the script.

TV PRODUCERS WORK IN MANY AREAS

documentaries

advertising

game shows

There are many roles for a producer – including weather checker!
It is my task to check the weather forecast during the day when shooting outdoors. Thankfully, the forecast is fine and sunny all day!

drama

news

soap operas

children's television

sports

talk shows

music television

animation

My favourite show!

How I became a producer

I always wanted to work in television. At school, I did well in English and I originally thought about being a television reporter.

At university, I did media studies as part of my Bachelor of Arts degree in journalism. While at university, I did work experience with a television production company. I also took on the role of producer/writer/director for some student films in my last two years.

After university, I got a job as a researcher at a production company that produced a science show called Tomorrow's Technology. Being a researcher on such a show was a huge learning curve. Right from the start I was able to originate and develop programme ideas, assist writers in preparing scripts, brief and organise the on-screen presenters and scout locations for stories.

Producing student films was a great experience.

Tomorrow's Technology, Episode 6 ... ACTION!

I've always loved capturing stories.

There was also a lot of legal work involved in regard to things like copyright clearances, intellectual property and music, appearance fees and issues relating to brought-in materials used for shoots. My time as a researcher for the show also saw me act in the roles of travel agent, meet-and-greet master, coffee runner and the "hire it in a jiffy" girl.

Being a researcher was an invaluable start in the industry. I learnt so much about negotiation, teamwork, crisis clearing and generally getting a project finished, no matter what the obstacles.

After working on Tomorrow's Technology, I worked as a freelance producer for a production house before finally becoming the producer for Purple Lava and Monster TV.

Purple LAVA

monster TV

Different kinds of producers

Staff producers are
employed on a continuing basis for a production company or television station. They are often assigned to a specific project or department. However, in small television stations, a producer will often float between departments and projects.

Independent producers put together
and sell production ideas to studios, distributors, network and cable television executives and publishers. Independent producers are responsible for the bulk of all prime-time television programming. An independent producer is not employed on a continuing basis – they work on a specific project or on a freelance basis.

Executive producers
are often less involved in the day-to-day production decisions than other producers. They delegate many production tasks to others and focus on developing new projects and concepts.

Dual roles combine the
role of producer, writer and/ or director. Writer-producer-directors immerse themselves in pre-planning and the day-to-day production process, almost totally controlling the quality of the original idea to the final product.

The independent producer pitches ideas to studios.

Executive producer

Co-executive producer
second in seniority to the
executive producer

Supervising producer
supervises other producers

Coordinating producer
coordinates two or more producers

Co-producer
works with other producers

Consulting producer
assists writers, sometimes specialising in
a particular subject

Associate producer
runs day-to-day operations

Segment producer
handles one segment of a program

Line producer
handles a practical aspect, such as sound or editing,
rather than creative content

Runners and production assistants
may be called on to do almost any unskilled task required
to help the production go smoothly

Depending on the
size of the project,
there are also other
kinds of producers
who manage, and
are responsible for,
specific areas of a
production.

*All types of
producers need to
be able to work
in a team.*

Qualities needed to be a great television producer:

- ✓ risk taker
- ✓ effective decision maker
- ✓ aptitude for solving problems
- ✓ ability to cope with changing situations and the pressures of tight deadlines
- ✓ good people manager
- ✓ creativity and imagination
- ✓ determination
- ✓ self-confidence
- ✓ excellent communication skills
- ✓ excellent organisation skills
- ✓ understanding of techniques involved in television production
- ✓ willingness to work on-location and in unfavourable conditions for long hours
- ✓ a sense of humour!

On-location shoots don't always go to plan!

my very organised filing cabinet

Some famous TV producers

Aaron Spelling – The King of Soaps
1923–2006

Aaron Spelling was listed in the Guinness Book of Records as the world's most prolific producer. He began his career as an actor in Hollywood in 1953, but quickly decided he was better off behind the camera, working as a writer and then a producer. His first major hit came in 1963 with a show called *Burke's Law*. During the 1980s he was king of the soaps, with his show *Dynasty* as a major prime-time hit. In the 1990s, he produced *Beverly Hills 90210*, *Melrose Place* and *7th Heaven*.

Reality TV gave a whole new meaning to the word "Survivor".

Mark Burnett – Mr Reality Television
1960–

Mark Burnett is a British-American television producer. He is known for introducing reality television as a genre to the USA. He produced the USA version of the series *Survivor* and the *Eco Challenge*. His company also set up such shows as *The Apprentice*, *The Restaurant*, *The Casino*, *Are You Smarter Than a Fifth Grader?* and *Pirate Master*. Mark Burnett has won two Emmy awards.

What do runners do?

A runner's job is often demanding and unglamorous. They are likely to spend time making tea and doing errands rather than greeting star actors! Based in studios, editing suites and on-location they work long hours and are often employed on a freelance basis for a short-term contract. A driving licence is essential.

Stages of production

Producers oversee
a project through various
stages of the production process.
If the production runs over schedule or over budget
in time or money, it is the producer who must step
in and decide what to do.

The production process can be divided into three
consecutive stages: pre-production, production
and post-production.

Pre-production

PRODUCER WORKS
WITH WRITERS

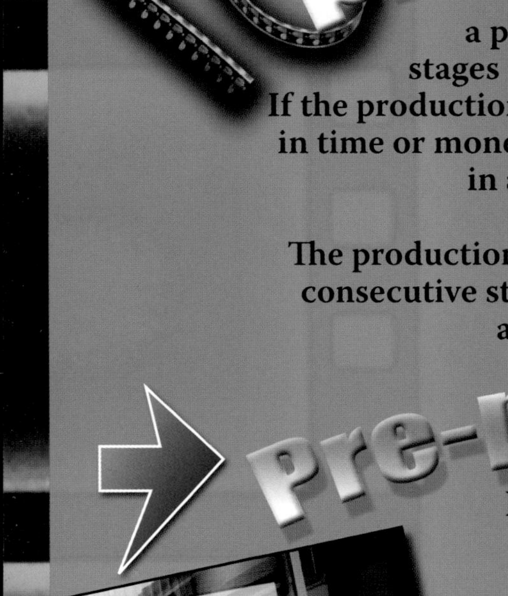

preparation of scripts → proposals → funding

preliminary budgets

synopsis ← preliminary budgets

treatments → scripts

hiring of talent

script breakdowns ← hiring of talent

production schedules ← script breakdowns

storyboards → legal requirements

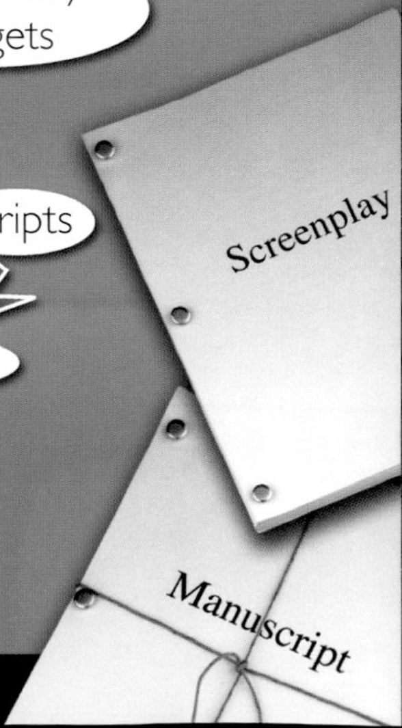

Screenplay

Manuscript

Production

PRODUCER WORKS WITH DIRECTOR

setup

rehearsal

filming

Post-production

PRODUCER WORKS WITH EDITOR

Colin is a wiz at sound mixing.

Post-production begins after the visual images and sounds have been recorded and includes:

editing
sound mixing
special effects

DIDYOUKNOW?

In the UK there is an essential directory of producers, technicians and facilities called Mandy's Film and TV Production Directory. It gives details of media jobs around the world. Have a look at **www.mandy.com**

15

Development timeline of a TV production

Programme idea →

The draft script

IDEAS, IDEAS, IDEAS

Script analysis

The script draft is examined in order of scenes (known as the running order) to give a possible duration of segments, settings or locations of shoots.

IT TAKES A LOT OF DRAFT COPIES TO GET TO THE FINAL PRODUCT.

Preliminary planning

The following issues are discussed:
• lighting, sound and set design
• cost • special equipment
• post-production techniques.

Final script

Rehearsals

The script is rehearsed in and out of the studio setting.

Casting

Camera script

This script includes details such as camera moves, positions and cues.

Specialist equipment

Sets are constructed, including planned lighting.

Technical run

This is a final pre-studio rehearsal. Problems are assessed, checked and solved. The studio is set up for lighting, stage design, sound equipment and camera equipment.

Production meeting

The director notes shot-by-shot suggestions, problems and changes. Technical facilities and special effects are discussed.

Camera rehearsals

Camera crew, sound crew and others follow the director's instructions.

Taping

The programme is recorded in sections or in its entirety.

Off-line editing

The director and editor examine the recorded footage. The director decides on the order of the shots, potential editing points and types of transitions.

On-line editing

Sequences are copied from the original tapes to make a show copy. Any corrections to the colour, balance or sound are made. Titles, audio effects, background music and special effects are added.

Show copy

The final version is checked and passed by the director and the producer.

Transmission

To archives!

The final version is copied for distribution and archiving.

Miriam is in charge of set design.

Pre-production meeting for Monster TV

One of the programmes my production company is trying to get to air, is a music and lifestyle show for 8-12 year olds, called Monster TV. We are still at the stage of securing funding to produce Monster TV; however we have secured funding to produce a pilot of the show. A pilot is a sample episode of the show that is market tested to secure sales.

Monster TV is in the early concept stage where the idea is still being worked out and the goals, strategies and look of the show is defined. Today, I am meeting with the executive producer of the programme to talk about the progress of Monster TV.

Production Goals and Objectives

Obtaining finance is easier when a project's goals and objectives are clearly outlined. Members of the production team also need to be aware of them to avoid confusion and conflicts in the production process.

Monster TV

Music Mayhem **Madness** Monster TV

Meeting for Monster TV

Idea: Monster TV is a one-hour programme of videos and interviews that revolves around the music, sport, art and gaming cultures. The format of the show has a collage-magazine feel with two studio presenters and a team of outdoor roving interviewers who are known in their fields of music, skating, surfing or gaming.

Production Goals and Objectives for Monster TV
1. Create a new and fresh way of presenting teenage television that reflects current trends.
2. Create informative and compelling viewing.

Possible monster TV directors, writers and presenters

Presenter shortlist
Kate Noon
Max West
Nick Spiteri
Lottie Charlton

Writer shortlist
Alice Ling
Eliza Easton
Jason Holper

Director shortlist
James Wilks
Kelly Van
Lloyd Black

skating

gaming

music

monster TV

AUDIENCE ANALYSIS AND RESEARCH

different people, different tastes

An accurate estimate of the size, demographic make-up and the needs of your audience are essential for funding and marketing ideas. Producers need to have an idea of the:

- size of the audience
- budget required
- interests of the audience
- age of the audience.

What do different people like to watch?

ADVERTISING

Television advertisers design commercials to appeal to different groups. For example, during cartoons and children's television shows, there will be lots of ads for toys, kids' movies and other things that appeal to children. Advertisers want to know that their ads will be seen by the people most likely to buy their product.

ADVERTISERS LOOK AT DEMOGRAPHIC GROUP STATISTICS SUCH AS:

- age
- gender
- income
- education
- culture
- language
- religion
- special interests.

What some people like on television ...

... other people dislike.

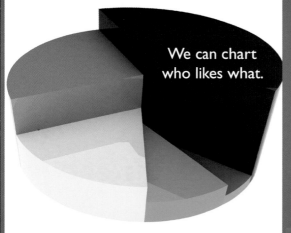

We can chart who likes what.

TESTING IDEAS

Commercial producers and distributors often rely on market research to estimate the size and the preferences of audiences. The title of the project, a list of key talent and the nature of the subject matter together with a synopsis of the show may be given to test audiences and their responses are recorded and evaluated.

THE PROPOSAL

Pitching a proposal can be nerve racking.

A proposal is a sales tool that describes the intended project, including all critical and unusual aspects of the production. It needs to be clearly written.

PROPOSAL REQUIREMENTS:

- concise statement – catch their attention
- outline the purpose and objectives of the project
- your approach, structure and style
- preliminary budget
- shooting schedule
- equipment list
- summary of credits and the crew's experience.

Celia Stewart

Hi Eliza. Don't forget the Monster TV proposal meeting tomorrow! C

Note to self: iron shirt for proposal meeting!

Monster TV
Music Mayhem Madness

Monster TV proposal

Producer: Celia Stewart
Director: James Wilks
Writers: Jason Holper and Eliza Easton

Monster TV is a vibrant and fast-paced show which captures the adventure and passion of youth culture. It is a music and lifestyle show, for kids aged 8–12 and showcases leaders in style and music.

Each episode consists of studio interviews and on-location stories, as well as music videos. The studio shooting schedule for the six episodes is two days. There are 12 different location shooting interviews that will be recorded over a period of six days. Research and preparation of the final scripts will be done within three weeks of the acceptance of the proposed treatment.

The budget will be approximately £200,000, depending on specific technical requirements of the script.

The format is magazine-style interviews and views interspersed with music clips.

Getting
something
on paper

monster TV

WE MEET WITH WRITERS FOR THE MONSTER TV PILOT

Scriptwriters are key in the pre-production phase. Once the producer has outlined their idea, the writer usually begins their own research, bearing in mind the producer's goals and objectives.

Keep your goals in mind.

A premise and synopsis and several possible story outlines are drafted before a treatment is prepared.

Scriptwriters usually determine the structural form of a project by writing a detailed summary known as a treatment. It lays the groundwork for a script and is written in the third person and present tense – much like a short story.

Treatments are a key part to securing funding, as they help everyone to "see" the project.

Once a project has secured funding and is given the green light to go ahead, the writer will then write a full script.

The script that follows, provides a scene-by-scene description of settings, action, dialogue or narration and functions as a blueprint that guides the actual production.

We've been given the green light on funding for a pilot!

24

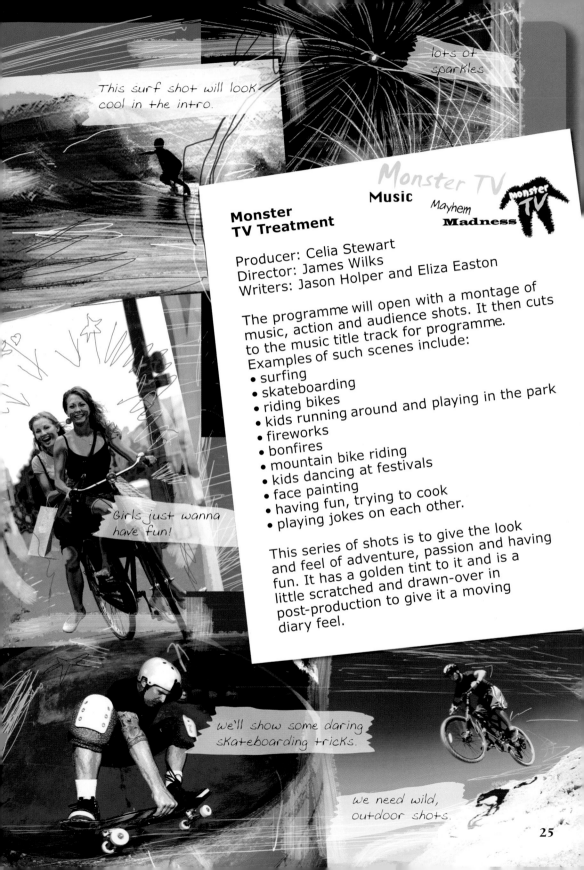

This surf shot will look cool in the intro.

lots of sparkles

Monster TV Treatment

Monster TV
Music **Mayhem** **Madness**

Producer: Celia Stewart
Director: James Wilks
Writers: Jason Holper and Eliza Easton

The programme will open with a montage of music, action and audience shots. It then cuts to the music title track for programme. Examples of such scenes include:

- surfing
- skateboarding
- riding bikes
- kids running around and playing in the park
- fireworks
- bonfires
- mountain bike riding
- kids dancing at festivals
- face painting
- having fun, trying to cook
- playing jokes on each other.

This series of shots is to give the look and feel of adventure, passion and having fun. It has a golden tint to it and is a little scratched and drawn-over in post-production to give it a moving diary feel.

Girls just wanna have fun!

We'll show some daring skateboarding tricks.

We need wild, outdoor shots.

25

Scriptwriting Basics

Scriptwriting can be divided into two basic categories:

- **fiction** (drama, soaps, miniseries, serials)
- **non-fiction** (documentaries, news programmes, live television, sport, talk shows, educational programmes).

Scriptwriting Formats

There are three basic script formats:

- full-page master scene
- semi-scripted
- split-page

Full-page master scene

This format is often used in single camera, drama and fiction-based programmes. The script is organised into scenes that are numbered in consecutive order. All visual and audio instructions fill the page in one column.

Jason is one of our talented scriptwriters.

Semi-script format

This form is common for productions that cannot be scripted, such as sporting events. It is just a rough outline that allows for greater freedom during shooting.

Who knows what will happen next!

Split-page script format

In this format, the visual information appears on one side of the page and the audio is on the other side. The Wildlife shoot for Purple Lava is in a split-page script format.

VIDEO	AUDIO
Images of lots of animals moving around the park. Fast pace, flashing from one image to the next.	High energy soundtrack including different animal noises. Include animal noises over soundtrack.
CLOSE UP shot of Kelly's face.	KELLY: I'M HERE WITH KEEPER ROBYN AND SHE HAS THE FANTASTIC JOB OF LOOKING AFTER THE TIGERS AT THE WILDLIFE PARK.
MEDIUM SHOT of Keeper Robyn feeding a baby tiger.	
MEDIUM SHOT of Kelly and Keeper Robyn.	KELLY: KEEPER ROBYN, TELL US ABOUT THE SPECIAL THINGS INVOLVED IN YOUR JOB.
WIDE SHOT of Keeper Robyn leading Kelly through the enclosure.	KEEPER ROBYN discusses her work.

Our director reads over every script carefully.

lunchtime with Keeper Robyn

Monster TV Shooting Schedule and Budget Breakdown

I now have a rough script for the six pilot episodes of Monster TV. From this I can devise a shooting schedule and make sure each episode comes in on, or close to, budget.

A shooting schedule indicates the total number of days of recording that will be required.

Music

Monster TV

Mayhem **Madness**

Title: **Monster TV**
Producer: Celia Stewart
Client: Giggler Productions

Date: 12-10-07
Director: James Wilks

1 Script (rights, research, writing, duplication) _____

2 Staging (sets, costumes, location fees, props) _____

3 Equipment (rental, lease, use fees) _____

4 Special equipment (mounts, aerials, jet skis) _____

5 Raw stock _____

6 Duping (time code copies, off-line copies) _____

7 Audio (effects, rights, fees, looping) _____

8 Music (fees, rights, performance) _____

9 Graphics (titles, animation, art) _____

10 Editing _____

11 Personnel (staff, crew, talent) _____

12 Travel (transportation, accommodation) _____

13 Distribution (dubs, promotion) _____

14 Postage/insurance _____

15 Other _____

Sub total _____

Overhead _____
Contingency _____

Grand Total = _____

Coming in on budget is a must.

Remember to work out how much each section will cost.

must book flights

PRODUCTION MANAGEMENT

When producers are managing a project, they need to break it down into parts so that it can be shot in the cheapest way possible. For example, if there are various scenes to be filmed on a ship, they will shoot all those scenes together on one day, even if it is out of order. This saves having to hire the ship for many days.

Script breakdown sheets and budgets help producers to manage a project within budget and on time.

Remember to book accommodation for the crew during the music festival.

DIDYOUKNOW?
BIG BUCKS

Movie budgets can be in the millions of pounds. Spiderman 3 had a budget of around £172 million — that's a lot of spidery special effects!

Studio shoot for Purple Lava

- ✔ Arrive at studio.
- ✔ Presenters go over their lines for the studio interviews.
- ✔ Meet the guests and give them a run through of what's expected.
- ✔ Meet with director and studio floor manager to discuss camera changes, issues and timetable for the day.
- ✔ Keep everyone on schedule and on track during the day's shoot!

DID YOU KNOW?

Over half of the UK's TV and film industry is based in London and south-east England.

The studio looks ready for shooting.

While Monster TV is still in pre-production, my other programme, Purple Lava, is in production. Today, we shoot the studio footage with presenters and guests for the episode that is to air this Saturday. Although it is only a one-and-a-half hour programme, shooting takes a lot longer as we set up different camera angles, shoot different segments, wait for guests and record some promotional footage.

A touch-up on Maddy's make-up.

Kelly goes over her lines.

MONSTER TV UPDATE MEETING

We have now decided on our presenters. We are having one boy and one girl studio presenter as well as a team of six rotation location presenters. Max and Lottie are to be the show's resident studio presenters.

Shooting of the pilot is to begin in three weeks.

Camera and audio crew have been hired.

The graphics team have made logos and promotional material for the show.

Max, our cool new presenter.

Peter has been designing our logo for Monster TV.

Lottie, our funky new co-host.

Max and Lottie, learning their lines.

We scored an interview with rock-chick, Alliyah.

MONSTER TV PROMOTION SHOOT

Outdoor location shots with the two presenters have been created for promotion. Both presenters have individually interviewed a rock star in the studio and a guest at a sporting event.

Studio sets are designed and made.

Theme music is prepared for the beginning of the show. A list of music we will use during the show is cleared in terms of legal permissions and copyright.

We want the Monster TV set to be fun: more colours please!

The director is putting together storyboards for the look of the show and how the studio footage is to be shot.

The director and I are pleased with how the presenters come across on camera. Both Max and Lottie looked relaxed and like they are having fun, which was one of the key objectives for the programme.

Max and Lottie are a match made in heaven!

33

Post-production

Editing

Editing is the craft of arranging, selecting, trimming and combining sounds and visual effects after recording. Editing can take place during production or in post-production.

A film editor works with the images, story, music, rhythm and pace, often re-writing the film during the editing process. It's the editor's job to make small snippets of film into a whole product.

trimmed shots

fade-out

Visual editing terms:

trimmed shots – unwanted portions can be removed from the beginning or the end of a shot

a cut – a direct, instant transition from one shot to the next

fade-out – the first shot gradually disappears and is replaced by blackness. When a shot appears from blackness it is called a fade-in

a dissolve – consists of an overlapping fade-out of the first shot and a fade-in of the second shot

transitions – a change of time or place from one shot to the next

Sound editing

Sound mixing is the process of blending together sounds or sound tracks. This includes transition devices such as fades, cross-fades and segues.

You need a good ear to be a sound editor.

DIDYOUKNOW?

Automatic Dialogue Replacement (ADR), otherwise known as looping, allows speech sounds to be added and matched perfectly to pre-recorded images. This means voice-overs and narration can be recorded and edited before the images are even selected!

There are three basic kinds of sound effects:

library effects – pre-recorded on CD and audiotapes
spot effects – specially recorded in the sound studio
actuality effects – recorded in the field

A voice-over artist at work.

Sound effects editors use a catalogue of sound recordings. There are several sound effects libraries available, the two most well-known being **Sound Ideas** and **The Hollywood Edge**. There are also online search engines, such as **Sounddogs**, which allow users to purchase individual sound effects from a large online database.

SPECIAL EFFECTS

Today, there are all kinds of production and post-production special effects that can alter pre-recorded images and sound or even create them from scratch. They can be as high-end as totally reconstructed digital images or as basic as make-up. Producers need to have an understanding of the limits and scope of these effects so they know which to choose in terms of budget and time.

One of the advantages of creating special effects during post-production is that it can save time and money, especially if a scene needs to be reconstructed and actors and crew called back to re-shoot.

Special effects are divided into seven basic categories:

1. digital effects – transitions, filters, compositing or grouping of more than one image, morphing of images

2. camera effects – fast and slow motion and single frame animation effects

3. optical effects – wipes and split screens

4. models or miniatures animation

5. physical effects — wind, fog, smoke, rain, snow, fires, explosions and gunshots.

6. make-up — ... transform an ... almost anything ... an alien to an ...

massive special effects

gruesome special effects using make-up

7. mechanical effects ...

... aboom? This include a mechanical props, guns, ... models, pyrotechnic and atmospheric effect. Making a car appear to drive by itself, or blowing up a building are examples.

aboom!

Chris, the director, is keen to incorporate some split-screen visuals for the on-location footage in post-production and also some freehand drawings over the footage to give it a diary-like feel. He has put together some examples with Jade the editor, and I like what I see. As long as they don't affect the budget, I'll tell them to go for it.

Remember to book the make-up artist for the next Monster TV episode!

Purple Lava at the Wildlife Park goes to air

It's 7 am on Saturday morning, and I wake up, switch on my TV and watch the Purple Lava wildlife special. The footage at the park looks excellent — not a hint of the trouble it was to shoot! The dusk footage with the animals at the end of the day looks great — like it was totally planned from the beginning!

As usual Purple Lava looks like a whole lot of fun without any evidence of the mad, crazy rush behind the scenes to get it to air!

Purple LAVA
Wake up! Purple Lava is on!

The sunset shots at the Wildlife Park look amazing.

the star of the show

Music Mayhem **Madness**

Episodes 1 and 2 of Monster TV pilot are tested

Monster TV feedback

A sample tape of the first two episodes of Monster TV is sent out to our executive producer, a sample test audience of teens and some television station executives who are interested in the show. We get all their feedback. They like the opening titles and think the pace of the show is good. They have a couple of suggestions for music artists and creative people to review. They generally really like the look and feel of the show. The response is positive and it fires us all up to finish off the other four episodes.

Poor
Satisfactory
Good
Excellent ✓

The sample audience enjoyed Monster TV.

Send Chat Attach Address Fonts Colors Save As Draft

To: CELIA STEWART
Cc:
Subject: Monster TV feedback
From: <Michael Anderson>

Dear Celia,

The interest from the sample audience was good! The station executives had a few overall comments. I'll send you more detailed comments in the coming days.

Overall comments
- keep the pace of the show strong and punchy with lots of scene changes and rest spots in the music clips
- great post-production graphics
- more interviews and profiles of young viewers

Great work!

SELLING A PROJECT

Once a programme is made, there are many different markets into which it can be sold and viewed. It is vital that producers have a basic understanding of potential markets for a programme.

There are many distribution and exhibition channels for programmes including broadcasting, cable, satellite, home video, multimedia, corporate and in-house.

Producers need to be familiar with the technology used by distributors so they can tailor the production to the requirements.

Producers also need to have an idea of the scope of profit for each market so they can promote the product accordingly. A production may not make it to commercial or cable broadcasting, but through marketing it can be very successful in the home DVD sales market.

It's all about making a profit.

TV shows can make money on the DVD market.

Shows that no longer air on television can also continue to make money on the home DVD market. Some television shows lend themselves to other money-making avenues via CD releases, books and merchandise.

DIDYOUKNOW?

On TV, in books and on shop shelves

Lots of television show personalities find themselves earning money from other ventures. Jamie Oliver has a television show and produces cookbooks, DVDs and merchandise such as cookware. He is also the face of Sainsbury supermarket's advertising campaign.

Maybe you could make Purple Lava: the book!

Follow these steps to become a television producer

1 Make your own documentaries or short films. Volunteer to be part of the production team for students who are studying film-making. Try and gain some work experience – it's a great way to make contacts in the industry and get your foot in the door. Enthusiasm and experience are really important.

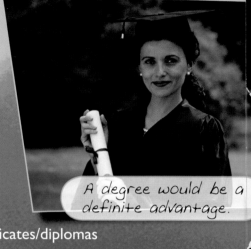

A degree would be a definite advantage.

2 There are no set educational requirements, but it's fiercely competitive and most new entrants have higher national certificates/diplomas (HNCs/HNDs) or degrees.

3 Degree courses in journalism, communications, media, and broadcasting are all useful. Check each course for A/H level, Diploma and GNVQ Advanced entry requirements.

Start writing your own short films.

Get your CV up to date.

4 It's not essential to have studied film, video or media production but it would be helpful to take a course that includes practical skills, work placements and the chance to make contacts. There are specialist courses in TV and film production available throughout the UK. Ask your Careers Teacher or Personal Adviser for more details.

5 New entrant schemes are also offered by organisations such as Skillset, the BBC and Channel 4. Join professional organisations or subscribe to publications from the media and film industry. Not only will this keep you up to date with news and events, it may also give you leads to work experience opportunities and occasions to make contacts.

6 REMEMBER: Most producers begin their careers as runners and then work their way up – don't give up. In a highly competitive industry, you must make your own opportunities. So, if you have an idea you are passionate about, get going, producer – start the pre-production process!

Don't just dream about your ideas – start producing!

OPPORTUNITIES FOR PRODUCERS:

Producers can work in a variety of jobs:

- full-time employee for a production company or a television station
- freelance or independent producer
- programme writers
- a technical editor
- work your way up to become an executive producer and oversee an entire project

OTHER RELATED AREAS TO CONSIDER:

Besides producers, the TV industry also employs:

- TV/Film Floor Managers
- Media researchers
- Radio producers
- Stage managers
- Entertainments managers
- Arts administrators
- Editors

Networking and having good working relationships is vital in this industry. Once you do land that all important first job, you will need to maintain good working relationships with others involved in all parts of the production process.

Useful contacts

Connexions / Careers Service and UCAS www.ucas.ac.uk
Contact your Connexions / Careers service for information on careers in this field, useful qualifications and possible college courses. They will be able to give you a list of all the university courses available.

Skillset www.skillset.org
They can provide information on career opportunities in the creative media industries including the role of TV producer. Skillset is the Sector Skills Council for the UK creative media industries.

FT2 www.ft2.org.uk
Film and Television Freelance Training.

Broadcasting Entertainment Cinematography and Theatre Union (BECTU) www.bectu.org.uk
373-377 Clapham Road, London SW9 9BT.

British Film Institute www.bfi.org.uk
21 Stephen Street, London, W1T 1LN.

The UK Film Council www.ukfilmcouncil.org.uk
10 Little Portland Street, London, W1W 7JG.

Further information

Large film and television companies often run internships and work experience programmes. For example:

The BBC www.bbc.co.uk/workexperience

Channel 4 www.channel4.com/4careers/4careers_new/work_experience.html

It is also worth seeking out independent production companies online and applying directly to them.

Glossary

archiving – to file away retrievable records

budget – an estimate of costs and profits for a project

copyright – a law which gives ownership rights to the creator of a product; forbids copying

demographic – a specific group of people (eg children)

documentaries – factual presentations about people's lives, real events or places

freelancer – someone who does not work on a regular salaried basis for one employer only

funding – providing money for a project

intellectual property – creative workers' rights that can be protected by copyright

merchandise – goods to be sold

morphing – changing into something else

networking – meeting people in order to share ideas and information

pilot – a sample episode of a television series

researcher – someone who investigates information

segue – to follow on to the next item without a break

treatments – a detailed summary of the story of a show

Index

WHAT'S IT LIKE TO BE A...?
PILOT
Elizabeth Dowen   Lisa Thompson

WHAT'S IT LIKE TO BE A...?
EMERGENCY NURSE
Elizabeth Dowen   Lisa Thompson

WHAT'S IT LIKE TO BE A...?
FORENSIC SCIENTIST
Elizabeth Dowen   Lisa Thompson

WHAT'S IT LIKE TO BE A...?
GAME DEVELOPER
Elizabeth Dowen   Lisa Thompson

WHAT'S IT LIKE TO BE A...?
ANIMATOR
Elizabeth Dowen   Lisa Thompson

WHAT'S IT LIKE TO BE A...?
BUILDER
Elizabeth Pickard   Lisa Thompson

WHAT'S IT LIKE TO BE A...?
SPORTS TRAINER
Elizabeth Dowen   Lisa Thompson

WHAT'S IT LIKE TO BE A...?
FASHION DESIGNER